tract

PROSE POEMS

Tract: Prose Poems
Recent Work Press
Canberra, Australia

Copyright © the authors 2017

National Library of Australia
Cataloguing-in-Publication entry
Title: Tract / by Prose Poetry Project;
edited by Monica Carroll and Paul Munden.
ISBN: 978-0-9953538-8-6 (paperback)
Subjects: Prose poems, Australian--21st century.
   Australian poetry--21st century.
   Australian prose literature--21st century.
Other Creators/Contributors:
   Carroll, Monica, editor.
   Munden, Paul, editor.
   Prose Poetry Project.
International Poetry Studies Institute, issuing body.
Dewey Number: A821.008

All rights reserved. This book is copyright. Except for private study, research, criticism or reviews as permitted under the Copyright Act, no part of this book may be reproduced stored in a retrieval system, or transmitted in any form by any means without prior written permission. Enquiries should be addressed to the publisher.

Design: Caren Florance
www.ampersandduck.com

This book was made with the support of the

 International Poetry Studies Institute,
CCCR, Faculty of Arts and Design,
University of Canberra
www.ipsi.org

Cover image: Dianne Firth, 'Road Across the Mountains', torn strip collage, 2012. © Andrew Sikorski, 2012.

recentworkpress.com

tract

PROSE POEMS

by the Prose Poetry Project
edited by Monica Carroll and Paul Munden

INTRODUCTION

Monica Carroll and Paul Munden

This book is the final part of a trilogy, a third selection of prose poems written by those involved in the Prose Poetry Project devised by the International Poetry Studies Institute at the University of Canberra. From all the poems written over the year, we have selected 98, representing 22 poets in the group.

In making the selection, we identified two distinct tendencies within the poems. Some dwell on a single moment, a recognised feature of much prose poetry throughout its history. Others, however, within a similarly small textual space, seem to treat time in a wholly different way.

As a structuring principle in the prose poem form, time as a single moment can give a sense of fixedness. Moments that are usually lost to the passage of time are transcribed into perpetually spun silk threads and webs. The prose poem rescues anonymous moments from slippage and names each instant through the compression of poetic form. Yet, more than this, the prose poem of a single moment can arrive into our lives at the right point and reveal a resolution or mood that we'd forgotten we lacked.

For the duration poems, there is rarely a single moment as such; if there is, it is elastic, sometimes encompassing years, even decades. Many of the poems amalgamate moments from disparate times in subtle and beguiling ways. Time is stretched beyond the initial observation or 'happening'. In some instances it takes on the quality of a mirage; time itself becomes an intriguing blur. Elsewhere its displacements are alarmingly precise, but all these poems explore the way in which we address the moment with reference to the past—and our notion of the future. The compact, free-flowing form of the prose poem enables the poet to surge from one temporal perspective to another, within a single short narrative frame. If time is stretched, it is also compressed into a remarkably brief space for the reader. We have the startling, disconcerting sense of experiencing time as if through a telescope from both ends at once.

We have chosen to present these two 'types' of prose poem as an interwoven sequence. Single moment prose poems are coupled with duration prose poems each speaking across the divide of pages. As with the previously published anthologies, this latest selection offers, we believe, a usefully focused way in which to encounter the work—and to ponder the extraordinary narrative and reflective capabilities of the prose poem form.

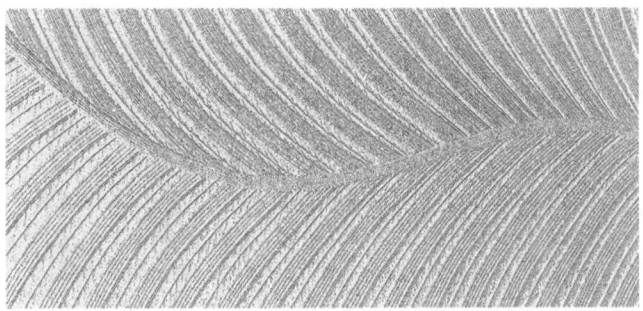

1

I am living on the outside of my skin. There's no easy way to return. I stroke this matter called me, dry and wrapped like fish awaiting the pan. I stare in at the vacant eyes, thinking of flesh. If I touched you you would tremble. If I kissed you you would gag. It's still me, but beauty has its own rules, and decorum. Look at me: viscera and blood, breath that goes wherever it will. I may never be touched again, but still I know more about its processes than can any one of you.

2

What he found, casually, was the shape of the shore, parsing its details like a languorous sentence. He stayed, although intending to go back, gathering a long breath and setting up camp. Night was a black expostulation; he cowered beneath it. But it grew familiar; the intractability of days became a relief. Driftwood and old sheets of iron made him a home. Jellyfish washed up so often they were soon a form of belonging. He found himself addressing the cosmos, at the same time realising his own absurdity. Years gathered in his body like stores of sea salt. He listened to his voice adopt the sound of breakers.

3

My dead cat is a bronze icon, but only in thought. Every evening he tells me what's wrong with the world, and his list is long. I imagine him on the bookcase standing next to Dostoevsky and Gauguin. He's an art critic as well as soothsayer; he doesn't like my paintings; his tail looks resplendent with its upward turn and polished sheen. He remains aloof and only eats air. I have come to depend on him and his advice. He bends stiffly and licks a damaged paw.

4

Water. Always trickling in my ears like the leavings of a fountain. It pools in my eyes when I sleep. I step across empty baths in winter. I pick old bicycles from the river, and shopping trolleys, and rusted anchors from mud flats when the tide goes out. In summer I watch dragonflies hovering over stagnant ponds hoping they don't drown. Mother told me never to fill the bath above the knuckle of your finger. And a cup of water's all that's needed to wash the plates. She drank from thimbles and trembled at waterfalls. We are mostly water, I told her one day. That made her shiver for a week. The rain gets in now, in the corner of the room, and the plaster is coming away from damp. I find my fingers pruning in dry air, a stream running down my back. I hear the ocean when I dream. The waves coming in and rolling over me and taking the smallest piece with them, again and again and again.

We no longer know our roles. The room's interstices, its strange comings and goings, dislocate us; what looked assured has dissolved in bright flusters. Even words have been debased and we want to speak them again. But light's now heavy as an arras; time slides on its silks, we're taken into an adolescence of feeling, and the future remains opaque. We wait for its drama to start, hearing actors tiptoeing behind the pleated grand drape. A wash of new light becomes every anticipation.

6

Stepping stones bleach in the indifferent sun, become mountains, crack to scree and, finally, sand. Frogs make way for lizards, rocking, throwing shapes in their jerkysmooth dancing. I see it all in the space of one deep drag on my first cigarette in three years, seven weeks, and two days. I'd add the minutes, but already a few ribs and the skull of some horned animal—cow? ox?—have appeared, barely casting a shadow. I flick the butt to anywhere and try to remember water: the sun's noon-high, and doesn't look like moving.

7

Raw silk, calico, sleeveless cotton in burgundy or cerise, a timeless blue skirt ... Her stage wardrobe is arranged with an algorithm calculated to make you forget. Stripes and checks in black and white, white and black (or is it navy?) ... Each day she appears as if fresh from the shops, charms you with the illusion of the new. The weather is glossed with the same, skilful repetition of the unique: every cloud a sweet nothing, every sunburst bright as your breakfast juice, every snowflake an unpredictable kiss.

It takes a year for the four white stripes on my nails to grow out. Evenly spaced transverse bands of white discoloration on my nail plate, I'm told I should think of them as my growth rings, my tree rings. But I bite them to the quick and cover them with nail polish, from cuticle to tip. When you take my hand, I curl my fingers around yours, hiding the ridges. Later, I push back my cuticle to examine my lunula for chalky striations, but I find only a waning gibbous.

And this dim-lit life is a glass vase in the making. Needs blowing and warming. She loads her rod with molten liquid from the furnace, rolling the orange glow at over 900 degrees in wet newspaper, until life begins to cool a little and harden. She doesn't wear gloves, dips it in powdered cobalt. She blows, then places her thumb over the rod until the glass begins to swell into a bauble, catching that air-bubble at its centre. Keep turning. Keep blowing. Find life's heat. Don't stop moving.

Down the lane, just yards from the main road, another small mews, its bright cottages all fitted out with grilles and shutters.

The same galleries in the museum I visited as a child: aeroplanes strung from the ceiling, a raised walkway to peer into the cockpits, a model of a water-raising device that appears to defy gravity, irrigates a miniature desert.

They are having to waterproof the pavilion, fill in the gaps with perspex, to deal with the unexpected sideways rain.

The vista of the park is cubed and squared, gridded; this is a building that lets in both light and air.

I count the sheep grazing in the pasture. I count the missing dead who they say are now living in paradise.

Bend around the time when no one is spooked yet by what will happen after. A rich man has a preference, a poor man has a prayer. A woman from the future has forgotten her oldest offspring and the spawn that's prostrate in the perambulator will become its own grandmother.

Huon Pine

It grew for centuries before he found it, sinking its feet into the cold southern soil, watching as the humans appeared, watching as the younger forests burned, and recovered, and burned again, as the seasons changed and the climate changed, as the protesters rigged hammocks in its limbs and as the loggers gave way. When it died, he hauled it down the rutted tracks, and carved it into boats and benches and guitars. The last small block he turned on the lathe. A golden bowl. He filled it with the shavings of itself. Sealed it with a metal grille. When he died, they took it to the dump. The tree is gone, and he is gone, and it is years since the shavings held their scent. I hold my face close to the grille, and breathe in what has no scent, a dead man's memory.

Those who don't know history are condemned to repeat it. Those who know history are condemned to watch it being repeated. Those who watch repeats can mutter along with the words. Those with watches can tell time. History isn't about time, and it's about time somebody knew that. There's a history of those who repeat condemnations. History repeats those who don't know. Replete with history, those who condemn are doomed. History is who knows? It repeats.

The last letter was written on a single leaf. Three words only, pressed into a book. Twenty years ago, on a rutted highway that had carried logging trucks, he'd stopped to help a stranger with a boiling radiator. Ten years ago that man had travelled half way round the world to be present at his birthday. Four years ago he'd nearly died repairing a snow-damaged roof. Last week he'd left a note about 'going into wilderness'. This was from the thick forest of his heartland, where his father had logged and made a whisky-fuelled catastrophe, written as snow etched his fingers, a way of saying that nothing more would be spoken between them. Twenty years dived into three words, and already it was pointless to reply.

15

After the apocalypse we sent in the dogs. First responders, sounding the air. They moved across the city, finding the signs, beginning to bark, beginning to point. Below them, cell calling silently to cell, lay the living. All day the dogs kept watch as we hauled rocks and scraped at the soil, our fingers bleeding, our shovels blunt. We pulled a child from where the school had been; a nun from the church. Three or four others we lifted from the heart of stone. We worked all day, pouring water on our heads, coughing up dust, the dogs urging us on, til they ran out of things to say. When evening came, they fell silent, and walked away, their tails held low.

Contracture

Her bass-clef hand is narrowing at the palm. Every few months another semitone is unreachable and she's hopping like ragtime to cover the loss. The surgeon gives her a leaflet, describes the zigzag incisions, says it means she has Viking blood, though she's never felt less red-headed. Back home she breathes blistered varnish, felted hammers with their faint, plosive dust, the acidulous brass of the pedals, the glottal silence.

Early on, they had spent a year in York, for his work. Tight with distaste and disappointment, she had paced the museum. Her memories are of bones—whistles, cracked from the legs of songbirds, a wishbone bridge for a Viking lyre.

On clear days your words are pocket-sized, even smaller than my small talk. In those quiet moments, I remember you breathing on my skin, a rush of adjectives in my ear as you slipped inside me. We are so often beyond words, I have forgotten how to speak your language. But when I see the sky from your balcony, I begin to understand your trajectory. Send me your silence and I'll confabulate it into the eleven words I need to hear.

I thought of the hallway where you stood for minutes after your husband's last phone call, in tangled conversation with yourself. When you turned you were white, as if already a ghost in your own place. Ten years later you answered the door in a dressing gown, pointing to the clock, saying 'It has betrayed me.' It showed the wrong time and its cuckoo no longer sang the hour. Webs climbed on your couch. Your scones were sweet and full, smothered in cream. You'd turned every picture to the wall. 'Look how beautiful he is,' you said, pointing to a photograph of a child, cut from a magazine. 'He comes every day— my angel.' And surely, as you spoke, a sound of wings outside the door.

19

Every week, she has trudged the quarter mile to church, taken up her solitary bench, opened the hymn book, and done her best. But every week there is a new fluffed note or erroneous chord that adds to the catalogue of mistakes forgotten by everyone—except her. And today the archival muscle of her fingers has reached its limit. In the shuffling silence as the congregation prepares to draw breath, there's a cracking of joints, and an inexplicable click of her teeth like a malfunctioning machine, followed by nothing.

A palimpsest of narrative thread pulled from the spool, a cotton reel of fibres, tightly spun to stitch ideas, a wefting pirn wheel, threadwound, winding the bobbin. Every day he was tempted to climb to the snowline; they said each ascent revealed yet another and another peak, layered like dog-eared pages in a once popular book of poetry, long discarded by changing tastes. Before the climb became a folly, he unwound himself, flagged down the flying shuttle and, stepping away from the loom, started to run.

Even if you don't believe that time is a river, there's no going back to that white slick of sand or the worn knotted rope over the waterhole that the boys swung and leapt from in summer, the hot ripples of brown shade and the treacherous tree trunk islands beckoning, until the prick of mosquitoes surrounded us at dusk.

22

Time was, you'd fall asleep on trains, wake up with a hangover to find yourself three, four, ten towns beyond your destination. You'd arrive home hours late, unsure where you'd been. After a time, you started waking up in strange houses, sometimes on a sofa, sometimes a bed, once in a large, white room full of silence and flowers. It was a knack you had. Now, you rarely wake up at all, sleeping across whole countries as strangers ignore you, bustling about their days. A friend thought he saw you in America, but couldn't be sure.

23

When he most wanted her love she was silent. The house's boards creaked under his feet; she had shifted; he'd not heard her; sunset was bleeding light. He thought of it pooling, of language that had gathered between them like clots, of feeling more fraught than he'd admitted. The light reminded him, although he was continents away from that past. There was an airy delicacy like gentle words. He'd gathered them, slipping them under his tongue. Yet they were hers, always. They meant welcome. They meant, do not speak for me.

Spook was three years old when her mother took off with a debt-collector travelling north. The world felt no great quake. Italian migrants still burned cane before the harvest. The night sky a blood orange. Brittle freight trucks kept rattling on slim rails. And signal bells clattered the moon. But Spook's Mama had gone. Nobody in town spoke bad about it. Except to say her Papa touched her Mama just twice in ten years, and both times he set a child in her. So Spook's Mama took the option when a new man spoke polite around her. Besides, the town was already dying. The crows and sparrows had lit out for elsewhere, sitting on the sills of southbound trains.

Spook's Papa just got on with his farming. Never saying much except for the names of machinery, pesticides, new sub-species of cane. One day, a decade into his lonesome time, the tractor broke down. The old John Deere. Spook's Papa took it as a sign. He let the farm go, told Spook's brother to watch out for her, and set to drinking like he was on the verge of some great discovery.

All he discovered was it was killing him. But he let the experiment run its course.

Spook couldn't really say she knew him. And she didn't recall her Mama's face, not in details you could offer to the police, or a priest in a booth. At least not when she was awake.

So Spook climbed into a 32-wheeler on the west side of town and let it go where it went.

25

Invisible stories and mythical monsters. Hymns, prayers and candles smoke in honour of the unknown. Look at us, scraping words together only to lose them again. We leave human skin and worn steps, move on slowly.

In those days you belonged nowhere. Whenever you could find a ride, you gathered your old suitcase and headed into distance. In the desert, still a boy, you were persuaded by a man from the side of the road and given cordial and sandwiches. His eyes studied you and his hands flexed uncontrollably. In Queensland you found yourself in a village where the locals got you drunk and, after much banter, strung a rope from a tree outside the pub, but you made it to a river. You climbed into the cabins of trucks and the carriages of trains. Once you woke up in a bedroom as a woman kneaded your back with strong hands. She said she wanted to marry you. Once you sat with linesmen in a forest and drank bitter tea. Ants climbed on your shoes and you helped them fell timber. In northern Western Australia you found an old shack and painted for a year— images of driftwood and views of coastal shrub. Someone joined you for two months but she hated the isolation. It was true you knew of no-one else within a hundred miles. For those four seasons you thought you'd settled. In cities you found the conversation tedious. Your childhood suburb in Sydney had been gentrified; you wouldn't go back. You rang your parents once a year but there were few words between you. Eventually your sister offered you a farm shed and a job as her gardener. That was thirty-three years ago, and frequently you look at the estuary next to her house, eyeing her boat. One day, you think, one day.

27

In the dark, I feel you reach for my hand as it lies, palm down, between our pillows. I'm not sure whether to leave it there and let you cover it with yours, or slide it away from your searching fingers. You once told me that love's isolation was beguiling, and so we have lived in this detached space for more than a decade. You interlace your fingers with mine, your palm heavy on my wrist. In the absence of light, I look for myself in our shared sleep.

His painting is about the tree that was there when he started painting the picture several months ago. He takes so long to complete his painstaking images that halfway through the process they felled the oak, which was growing too large for the garden, blocking the light and shading the house. Some of the pencil marks showing where the tree was remain on the surface of the painting. It is about absence, about the passage of time, about the way the sunlight moves acrosss the brickwork towards next door.

(for Mark)

He was an animal crawling in tunnels under earth. The periscopes he made reached into treetops and he watched the birds there. Their scurry and fluster delighted him and he adored the expansive mime of their song, tuneful thought elaborating their repeating visions. How their breasts plumped; how their beaks opened like the mouths of thinned trumpets. He examined his pale skin and its sores, wondered if sunlight would, after all, become him. And might he also declaim? He dusted his manuscript, searching for a place to belong.

Once her neighbour had died, his son cut down the oak trees. Five of them shaded the back of the row of terraces and once they were felled, light flooded in. No birdsong. There were no acorns to collect in September and wind hit the back of the houses from the valley like a scream. Alice had loved the trees, their stunted trunks and ability to cling to life when circumstances were thin. She sketched the trees from memory but could not catch the way the sunlight had dappled the windows or the smell of them. That resinous, earthy smell that signalled Spring.

It's the light that bounces off the cracked surface of the canal, that scatters against the daubed walls of the buildings. It's the streets shifting, improbably, under our feet. Subtle but certain, reminders that all we have is fleeting. We mail each other postcards, tiny gestures toward permanence. We tell each other this will never change, even as buildings slide under the sea, even as our postcards crumple and blur.

At the edge of the field, children cup water in their hands, stuff their mouths with watercress, blow sand into each other's eyes. It's a sport of sorts, a competition they don't realise they've entered. Later—maybe hours or maybe decades—their mothers will sit them down, discuss performance, suggest tactics for the next round.

Your words propel from your mouth electroplated against the power of tears. They tarnish in the microsecond it takes for them to travel from your mouth to my ears. They clatter into my hands where I hold them and although I can see with my own eyes the verdigris forming at the corroded tips of tines and blades, can smell the acid bubbling out from the inside, my first thoughts are of how to make something beautiful out of them. Something that will last. As fast as I can bend them into shapes, the shapes dissolve and tattoo my hands with the words *caution*, *fail* and *go*. This cycle of metallic utterance and acrid scarring continues until not even I can hope.

The strangeness between parent and child. Adult to adult now, almost matched. She reduces you with a gesture, with a phrase. Reminders of you before it was you. Reminders that once you were completely loved. Once sang yourself into language, while she sang in turn to you; once sang, conducting the world with small inquisitive hands. The memory is more than you want to endure. You stand taller, forget the toddler self who in a guilty corner is still trying to work it all out.

In the brief caesura between breaths, my head floods peach; a decanting of orange behind closed lids. Our sweat mingles in whorls in your chest hair and I swim beneath you, legs slipping up around your waist, urging you deeper into me. The afternoon presses on us, a double fermata of covetousness and dreaming. You push back my hair from my face, but I'm never sure what you are searching for.

Tablecloth on the table. Union picnic day. Sun is too sunny and gum trees thin. Cordial from the cooler tap runs warm. Hoops and skipping ropes for the children. Conversation and beer for the grown-ups. Sometimes a guitar and microphone start. Other years Santa rolls up on the back of a flat-tray. The happiness is shifty; there was never innocence. A can catches hot fat running through the bbq sinkhole. Onions smell better than they taste. The lake beckons, promising cool relief. Men stand wide-stanced, hairy arms crossed. Had they read the graffiti on the cinder block toilet wall yet?

The past is a list of forgotten possessions and events; my love affair the beginning of heartache. Oh how my ears ring and my joints ache when I pass you on the street. I wish I wish I wish I could move time forward and the past back. In my little world I am all there is and all there could be. I would race myself to heaven, sing in silence and make your life hell.

At the first cut, he didn't yank back the neck far enough to snap, and the sick ram scrabbled away across the slaughter-pen, bleeding out, till its stifle and hock buckled. The anatomy lessons stuck. Later, in Jesselton, he was the one with science enough to be summoned by the surgeon. The girl had multiple stab wounds, was opened up. They located the many, glancing intestinal perforations by the white heads of parasites, worming up.

when they put me through the mill, words came out, some meditative, some loving, some detailed. they threw the meditative words on the scrap pile, chewed the words of love like tobacco and spat them out after lunch. kept the details.

Birch trees in rows: like potatoes, like wheat. In summer they have a more louche air, clustering around the bar, setting up a card game. Now, winter-naked, they are more formal, more forlorn. You touch one with open hand, the way you touched your mother's coffin, the way you cupped the small dead bird before burial. The ordered and the lost, together in one presence.

The room leant on them until light was a press of decisions and years. They stood in their histories as in clothes, straightening themselves. Words reminded them that what might be spoken was less than they'd thought. He remembered a long-stemmed flower in a vase, so many years ago—how it seemed to curl into its own beauty. They'd not known themselves, though believing they knew. They'd not been able to say what was between them. Light sieved until it banished, like a dissipation of belief. And in all the time since, still that room stood within him, merging with rib cage and breast bone.

In digital mineral formations, the structures are no less ornate and astonishing. If you go down to the lower levels, you will find these words squeezed into narrow columns which had been spread wide as fields when they lived on the surface. Up here, only fenced distance encloses and surrounds, faintly containing a narrative of tracts. As each new layer is sent, the older ones begin to fold and become the roots of the new in the rocks of earlier beginnings. From down there, the trees seek liquid, nutrition, while up here the leaves excite and stimulate, become the earth in which the next one will grow.

43

Night finds it ever more difficult to get out of bed. Tries it legs first (but then how to move the torso?) and tries it torso first (but then legs lie sullen on the sheets), and gives up, waits for the nurse. Age is no-one's friend. Night finds digestion more trying, bladder more demanding, bank balance more slender. My own delicate soul grows raddled, my cheeks drawn. Age. It lies in wait, irrespective. Even rosebuds study their faces in the mirror, all dread.

Mounds of soil tremble in recognition as first my heel then the sole and last the toes of my feet press onto them—they carry my weight as though they carry their child—their children are bleeding back into the dust from whence they came—waves of gravity soar one after the other in a crescendo of space colliding with space—after a while Einstein puts down his bow and whistles the harmony—for a hundred years the heat rises, the soil becomes darker, the notes more discordant till the woodwind run out of breath—there is a single note left rumbling in the ground, an echo from the beginning—the stars tremble in recognition.

Each year, there's always a moment when she holds the feeling again: separation; the abnegation of touch—in a supermarket, perhaps, when she's handling a firm green crown of broccoli; walking under tall oaks that are gathering shapes from the sky; standing next to a bonfire, burning the old things. Or shucking oysters in a foreign city, cutting and lifting hinges of shell, revealing muscles of flesh. She thought of herself then, exposed, unguarded, and his words like a blade. She walked to a bar and drank twelve Camparis, one for each year.

I'm planting for the next people now, hoping they'll believe this has always been so 'cottage-garden', so carelessly crafted. The clay will squeeze the annuals upright long enough for the auctioneer's hammer, the pungent mulch freshly shovelled should disguise the exhaustion beneath.

When did I grow so bored with it all? Windflowers bobbing and bearded irises; cuttings gift-wrapped in gladwrap by a mother-in-law; bulbs in brown paper bags in the fridge; seeds, small as dust, catching in the corners of their paper packets; sticky forget-me-nots, not forgotten, just neglected to death. Now, I am strenuous. Next autumn, when the first early frost crisps the lawn yellow, a stranger's child will slip, running unknowing for the swing that hung from someone else's ancient plum, the one we cut down to make way for the deck we did not use.

Of all the new purchases filling your basket, I sensed your favourite was the fist-sized tube of startling orange—an impulse, an excitement among the necessary supplies—so that now I picture it in pride of place, there on your workbench with all those colours of the sea, your hand straying towards it with a sudden highlight in mind, and before I know it I am squeezing a thick splurge from the metal tube onto your palette, daubing an intrusive *me me me* on your thoughts.

Our tongues were fat from eating hedgerow mulberries, blackberries, sloes, damsons sour as lemons, the first bilberries of the season. Fingertips and lips stained purple. Our Tupperware boxes leaked juice-trails down Boundary Lane lined with rose bay willow herb and cow parsley, as if we were carrying a dismembered body home that afternoon. I was reading Laurie Lee, Heaney and Lawrence. It was high summer but the season was on the cusp of something momentous. At night we slept closer together: four sisters blowsy with heat and sunburnt shoulders. We were skinny as wild cats and our feet were calloused from wandering barefoot for weeks. Soon Lily would slip on borrowed stilettos, smear her cheeks with rouge and be gone forever. Mother sterilised Kilner jars in the oven, pursed her lips. She filled a larder with the summer's glut then slow-cooked meringue, brittle with resentment and sugared love that mixed together behind closed doors. It can all happen in an instant, she said, darkly. I'd no idea what this meant, just yet. These were days of rust and nettles.

The buttons on your coat, the colour of your eyes, the way you smile at the world you don't really know; hope is a way of travelling but you don't yet know that the hand being held out is not offering friendship. Hand over fist, hand over mouth, hand over the money, handouts are not for the likes of you. You give but you can't take back, your sighing is as worthless as the buttons on your coat.

For the first fortnight she drank only rainwater, drawing it from the tank, loving the satin texture on her tongue. The fifteenth day something swam to the surface of her glass and from then on, bore water was the only option. Gradually the taste of iron, a sandpaper flow, became her taste. The old tank dozed under its rambling rose, the hills and valleys of its corrugations becoming the domain of lizards and red backs, the subtle drip of its tap drawing snakes and roos to the back door, while the windmill turned, while from the kitchen window she watched the tank like she'd watched the disappearance of love.

It was like holding water in her hands and, surprisingly, seeing it stay there. She watched its flickering surface and thought she might swim—if the pool was larger; if it left her disbelieving hands and tumbled into an attractive blue. Yet she'd never learnt the skill. Bodies of water threatened drowning and now she wondered what she held. It was, after all, just an idea of love—something she might keep and surround. But his letters tumbled with saying and wouldn't be contained. She could not swim in such words.

The long brown river carries the sweat and dirt of thousands, thousands of bodies walking through its waters, thousands of clothes dipped and scrubbed and rinsed free of stain and smell, and given this country's laws, there rest on its bed the bodies of hundreds of unwanted newborns, more female than male, from the bundle slid into the cold at dawn, to bones in the silt. The laundrywomen, their eyes tearing, say onions grow upstream, and maybe they do, but that is not why the women cry, why for the rest of the day they touch and touch everyone they meet, brushing back a stray hair, squeezing a shoulder, loitering in an embrace. If they lie awake after midnight, they'll taste despair, metallic on their tongues, and come morning, their fingers will tremble with it.

In this room we never get clear of the buildup. We don't know ourselves under the thickness of being. The papers I sort endlessly, without purpose. The clothes piled over the backs of chairs hunched like imprisoned animals. The shelves covered in small objects we never meant to keep. You look away, preferring to leave things to time. I move things around hoping for clarity. Only after the cat knocked over the yellow vase, a wedding gift I thought lost long ago, did we begin to think of locking the door and leaving it behind.

It was growing up that soured you. The things you'd not expected. All those rules, the sudden chill of change, and with it your knowledge of time, and how it keeps breaking its banks, and how the trees keep half an eye on the flow. We walked up the hill today, looking for mushrooms, and finding, at every corner, the hum and glow of new leaf, new-born magnolia blooms haloed against the light. Startled by beauty you had not imagined, you reached for me, sweetly, you threw back your head and hallooed the sun.

Sky flooded the room like a watercolour's wash. 'Forgive me,' you said repeatedly, as if a motif. Twenty years had come to this. A walled garden below, an assignation's pencil scrawl, body boards cramming the room's corner. You were swimming out, hugging a board. When your glazed eyes rolled towards me I would have lifted you up, but 'not yet' were the paramedics' words. I believed the sea had siphoned you away—on a shingle where pebbles were inquiring eyes. In this room with the heaving blue of words.

I carry clouds, storms on my shoulders, cowls of thunder framing my face. When all becomes script and sigilla, it's a time for scholars, and I have mapped the year with isobars, occluded fronts, peacock tails—an Arcanum of alchemical meteorology. I read forms of beasts, tracing tracks with unsure fingers as herds emerge from margins, a fog of hooves and steaming breath. For all that's lost in translation, new abstractions arise, signposts to unexplored terrain. It's the longest November on record, and the night sky is bright with swans and eagles, the sea with foaming horses. Fire, Water, Earth, Air: as storms break, I wish you favourable winds.

Our bodies, drifting. The sky, drifting. The boats weaving between us, oblivious. Salt in our mouths, in our eyes. We swam until we were tired, and then we drifted again. Our arms remember, our legs, our skin. The sea. Our first home and our last.

When Alice was a child all the clouds in the sky were beasts and creatures—minators and centaurs, winged angels and angry giants. Thunder was a wardrobe being thrown across the heavens. Now, for days on end, the weather is calm; a wintery calm when the world is cotton wool in the morning and all afternoon the trees are still, like a woodcut or etching. Alice thinks of unexplored terrains today and longs for a desert, a view of the ocean, somewhere with a long vista. She remembers Constable country, his skies and low horizons. She remembers seeing Turner in the National Gallery and bursting into tears. There's a cold front rolling in from the Atlantic and things are shifting. Her neighbour's farm is full of rescued peacocks, calling to each other, shaking out their beautiful tails.

As you leave, the garden sighs a restless stillness—climbing plants stir their tendrils and groundcovers crawl, snails gather, the ripening of raspberries and rhubarb can be heard. You grab my wrist to stem the flow of words that hang like under-ripe figs waiting to be pecked by birds.

One day when I was nine or ten I went for a walk with my granddad on Patea Beach, and as we came around the head he saw the face of the cliff fall away from the cliff to stand, upright, beside it. I didn't see it but he was shaking, weird to me, and there was the broken cliff.

This morning I missed my bus and walked alone for the first time in ages, relieved by April wind on my eyes which I strained reading comments in the dark as my son went off to sleep. Someone was explaining that as we do not know our great-great-grandparents, nor our great-great-grandchildren, there's no real reason to care what happens in a hundred years' time. And there's a certain lightness to imagining that—the freedom of unloving, dumbness going on like a bell already rung.

You wake as a young boy runs to your bedroom, bewildered by his dream—and with a burning question: 'Is there a city where the streets are made of water?' You smile, nod. Affirmation is easy: it's in the surge that pulls you towards the Accademia Bridge, the smell of green canals, the lapping bells ... Harder to grasp is how knowledge can be a gift, like the hand of a stranger, instantly a friend; lightning's sudden description of the lagoon. Some days you still feel that gentle rock of water underfoot.

Opening the folder he noticed the sealed envelope, with an inscription in pencil: 'do not open until 2050'. The folder would never have been consulted—marked 'cuttings from gardening magazines' it was crammed with columns about the care of roses. She'd been well-known as a flower painter but critics' estimation of her work had faded. He slid a finger and pulled blue sheets of notepaper free. When had she inserted this letter? 'I'm not who I say I am. I killed my brother when I was seven and he was three. I need to tell someone, anyone … though, now, surely it cannot matter? I stole my family history from a friend killed in the war.' He tore the words into fragments, thinking of forty years as a manuscript curator, keeping and ordering his mother's exemplary life. He went home and began to burn her paintings—ten that evening. In coming weeks he'd burn a hundred more.

All the girls with long hair and big bottoms and bottomless glasses bumping into each other and shifting nothingness on its axis, momentarily. They fling their bodies in reckless cartwheels creating a no-fly zone for other punters. The night ends in tears when a head bang connects with her nose and their circle collapses in on itself in the final encore.

Fixity

Algorithms insist that this image on my screen has not altered by one pixel, that the burn of your cheek is as fresh, the bleed of sweat on your mare's flank is as dark, her eye as rolling. I'm almost out of the frame, one sandalled ankle in a stirrup. The stirrup is the stirrup it was, exactly. Your hair, I see now, is more halo than afro but afro or halo enough for a white girl with thin, red arms, hauling in a sweating mare with rolling eyes unaltered, though the horse must have been for the knackery these forty years, or tractored into a pit on the bottom paddock.

In the span of ten minutes you can mount and dismount an elephant many times over. You can sew up the mouth of a full sleeping bag or run two four-minute miles and have a heart attack. But if you have two contractions you're still not in labour. And you cannot make and drink a cup of tea.

Cold harbour decoy, someone else's pictures of someone else's life: the person I used to be. Blurred stories from elsewhere, small people in the distance who grew up and moved away, stopped holding my hand or believing what I say. There are things I would like to forget but can't, certain haircuts and clothes, old girlfriends and cars, places we never wanted to live in, stored in cyberspace and memory sticks, online photo albums I don't know how to edit or amend. My memory is fading, like several of the actual photos hanging on the wall.

It's as if the air itself could catch fire. The sea is a blazing mirror, the clouds are shoals of fish, hovering, and the dancing tendrils of reed are the rain that refuses to fall. We cast out to the horizon and wait for the change.

These fish bones. They fill your kitchen with the memory of salt and taste of kelp. As you listen to the shipping forecast, some stick in the throat, some spread out on your plate like something found in an archaeological site, some send you coughing and running for the phone. Some are so sweet you spend a Saturday making a fish bone and feather necklace. You wear it to a wedding with a blue silk dress and calfskin slippers. One morning you head for the Northumberland coast. You were there when life was sweet and rockpool clear. Turning through a stone arch, you drive down a winding road to Craster, its harbour a tiny semicircle of stone. Those silver darlings drip oil in the blackened sheds. Kippers packed in a barrel. They keep your lost love preserved all winter.

We played Hangman. Your stick life granted by a single unguessed word. The chaotic clatter of being hanged makes each death a miracle. So much depends on gravity. You asked for gold, not sand, in your sack of counterweight. Going out in style, you told me. I stuffed it with gramma.

70

A British soldier walks out of Grandma's closet, walks down Netheravon Road towards Sealand, vanishing in the shadow of the sodium street lamps. She tells us this before dinner, explaining why she wants to leave early. She is not distraught exactly: she's lived through the War after all; knows what these blooded beaches can account for; what a purple sky used to mean. But someone will have to take her home. Still, there is little point all of us decamping: the old chalet is paid up for the weekend and it is only Saturday. Flight can wait. Meanwhile, twilight. Chicken wings on the barbecue, Lee Kuan Yew on the radio, exhorting Asian values, hard work. Hard water comes out of the taps, this close to the sea, chalks our tea and salts it, makes it taste of old bones brewed too long in one of Grandma's double-boiled soups. She's almost forgotten she wants to leave now, watching her grandsons scamper across sandy grass with makeshift harpoons fletched from satay sticks and straw. Or did she leave at once, her lingering a wished-for, fashioned fancy? Years hence, Grandma long since gone, lovers end their lives in Chalet M. SARS prospects quarantine in the bungalows. Invisible hands trip a novelist, near the morgue of the old hospital (now hotel). She tells me this before dinner, with the same equanimity, the same grey in her fringe, her tongue-sharp Cantonese. Something about how memories groove. Our repetitions bleed through. Perhaps we scar time. We who live stories left behind, who try to forget fear. Marching without looking down or back.

'Do you usually have difficult veins?'—the nurse's brows are furrowed, one latex-gloved hand resting lightly on my left arm—as though I haven't spent years trying to teach my veins to behave properly, the flesh above her hand is already turning a familiar greenish blue and the other arm a greenish yellow (partly in mortification, partly in anticipation)—'Let's try the other arm'—oh yes, let's try that other path, there seem to be fewer pot-holes that way, never mind the rising river the birds flying in the opposite direction the boulders lurking on the slope the hospital still on the other side of the mountain—it doesn't sting anymore, so I stare at her bent head, a glossy black the colour of raven's feathers—ravens are meant to mate for life, ravens are meant to circle the sun bring good luck win the war be shapeshifters be gamechangers—her hairline is damp with sweat, my hands have gone numb, her fingers are ice-cold, my body is an utter failure, again—'I'm sorry, you'll have to come back tomorrow.'

In other universes, the parts that actors play are their real lives. They do not know why they speak to themselves in dramatic monologue. The people you slept with have traded places with the people you wished you'd slept with. The dog you owned as a child appears on TV as a Sunday morning cartoon, beloved by children everywhere, and lives in the memory of adults as nostalgia warm and pure. Narrative time gawps at an empty plain and waits for movements of the sun. Unbroken attention spans hold on and hold on and hold on ... In other universes, each conclusion is the right one. All suspicions have been confirmed. Each decision has been made, each chance taken. Each possibility, no matter how outlandish, is achieved. Each sperm and egg are children. Each bomb dropped does not explode. Every indiscretion has been discovered. Every daydream lives and aches and draws pay. In other universes the molecules that comprise your body differ by one. Cancer can be a good thing. Gods pray to humans, and humans pray to dust. In other universes, the fears you wake to have manifested, or remain ideal. However, their sum never diminishes or expands. In all universes, this is a constant.

You mention Palestine and I leave the room. You raise that tricky crossword clue and I offer a solution. When I say rape, you say it's complex. When I say jazz, you say it's joy. The soldier is lurking in his uniform. He performs acts he'd never dream of while wearing jeans. We are bent out of shape: words don't go far enough.

Installing

Jón Páll Sigmarsson's first installation is a mobile phone standing 12 feet high. You type the letter A by pulling down a lever which takes all your strength. Activate letter B by lifting a 30 litre bucket of water from a shelf at chest height. Clock letter C by sawing through a 40cm log with a bow saw. A message can take an hour. The exhibit relays what you've written to a real cellphone which sends the message, though there might be network problems. Sigmarsson's work will be tremendously popular, the gallery owners tell me.

The difference between shame and guilt: eating a flower without knowing its name; eating a name. To be a saint; to be conditioned to vexation, being watched watching. From the top of the hotel you cannot see the lobby, but there's a clear shot across the street in the room where the French theorist might have died laughing. How is the box any bolder clad in cloves or cinders? The word deconstructed, as the weather threatens to break into dance. Waltz with risk, whatever your flag. But someone spent so much on this palisade!

Old photographs are constellations, discrete patterns in space. This one, I think of as Equus: seven monochrome images of a Dartmoor pony, my parents, my aunt, me aged maybe two, rising on the summer horizon. I trace their pattern through imprecise cartography, degrees worn blank on a hand-me-down astrolabe which, for all the advances in technology, I learnt to read from Chaucer, leading my fingers through the umbra versa, the Cercle of the Dayes. Gestures appear young and easy, but there are no reactions from these neutrons, white dwarfs, black holes: these shapes map my first memory, and in the years between, light has travelled 3,233,174,989,935 miles.

It was a cold and windy night, a half-hearted moon drifted lazily through the trees, the wind-shaken leaves casting shadows across my face. You said I didn't need a Halloween mask, nature had done enough; falling, hitting my head on the cracks in the concrete, I had lain there, breath and flesh and bone, cold against the stone—it bled when it cracked but as I lay there catching a breath I thought, I have no further to fall. Then when the guisers came, dressed as ghouls and witches and hammer house horrors, I frightened them with my bloody face, they didn't challenge with their trick or treat threats, no promises of a song, though somewhere in the distance I thought I had heard a lone wolf howl. It was a cold and windy night, under the gaze of a half-hearted moon.

A cygnet was brought in from the lake today, its neck broken by a pure bred dog. I read about the bird in the blue room. I hear swan song, a keening that rises from the disco city and the silver banks beyond it. The journalist is blue and underpaid. Where, she writes, did the rushes go? The freeway casts shadows on my blue room walls. I read somewhere the world itself is residue. The sound of blood in transit is oceanic—I am small again, holding a shell to my ear. The cygnet was buried; the dog put to sleep. Cold stars turn on at the end of blue days.

79

I can't sleep—please ask the rain to fall more softly, the lady to cut more quietly, the runner to tread more carefully as she winds her way through my parietal lobe.

Every window is open at the same precise angle, each frame a sundial telling the distance from then to now. You still cup your cigarettes to your palm, take furtive hummingbird pecks, as if your mother will appear round the corner. The shop's boarded up, its bubblegum machine as empty as a cage, though you can just make out the prints of tigers, elephants, penguins; still smell the popcorn and astringent pop. And when you look up, you see a young girl in a white blouse and striped tie, hair like ropes and ivy, waving to you, waving to a stranger, waving to passing ships, and singing, loud, but out of tune.

When you touch me, so determinedly, screwing your courage to the sticking place, I fail. Words fly from my grab-bag of chance. Some reach my tongue. But this is no time for speech. You kiss me, and my words are occluded. That's a big word for a little girl, you say. But all I tried to say was no.

The sweater in the drawer, picked out in green thread; two leaves dried in a book. There were three of them in a country lane in Devon, a bicycle flashing past—though the crossing had seemed deserted—a letter's second page wafting and dropping in the breeze. He should have kept it, he thought, but they folded it three times and left it on a stile, a rock holding it in place. He saw that long 'feminine' loop of the writing, with ornamented descenders: '... as if time has never thought of us; as if, together, we are the cocoon itself'. His two companions married and the boy rushing by on the bike became a doctor. He wondered how he knew that, in the tail wind of memory. He looked towards that landscape and suddenly knew the girl.

Words are symmetries cut in silent cloth. A design on the earth. A net to hang the tiny necks of solitude.

Putting it to wash, he finds his old maroon t-shirt still holds the ghost of sticky white tape that fixed the electrode to his chest, a fibrous square with a penny-sized absence at its centre somehow meshed to the cotton, even after all these years. He closes the door and watches the machine kick suddenly into reverse—as does the ambulance, taking him back from city hospital to rural dark, the blue light outblinking the sleepy village. He's slumped at his desk, mumbling answers to questions, questions, watching the empty bottle reacquire its pale orange allure, and feeling the strange jerk of his body twisting the child-proof cap of the plastic container into place. Then there's another kick, a further reverse of the machine, back into the future, saving him from himself.

Crackling noises in the dense weeds. Another tree has fallen, while the weekend wandered by, and shocked birds are fluttering around their broken nests, their broken eggs. I am nothing but desire, every synapse attuned to the sensations that career around my skin. Nothing will satisfy. Burning, burning, I take an axe and get to work on the low branches, on the embarrassed roots. It could take weeks but I have everything it takes and more. Watch me go.

Trees closed their faces. In the orchard a basket stood empty. He pushed past thick memory and lowered his feet into the creek. Runnels of sand, old explosions of thought—what had he believed? He turned towards voices: two girls who were arguing. The breeze failed to feel like yesterday. The old house was an emblem of its own neglect. He felt culpable, although he had left. Because he'd left, he felt implicated. Broken forms offered no consolations as he tied shoelaces and thought about when he first decided to leave. It had been a Sunday, after church, and Geoff had hung himself from a wire in his father's hay shed. He'd left no last words.

And to my listeners across the country, I am humbled and honoured to be your correspondent. We all know that for every listener who loves me there's one who'd see me in my grave, and I would honestly fuck every one of you if only to stop the trolls. Meantime dear listeners let's take our seats and wait calmly for whatever is next on the bill.

In the blue light of bending metal, time stops. You notice: the winter lake of skate-cracked glass; Constable fields redrawn by Matisse; the censer arc of the swinging key fob. These are the pictures you will cut carefully around, store in an envelope, in a desk drawer with bills and contracts. Your grandchildren may find them, but will not understand how everything stopped but the dash-cam that kept recording, and how the whole sky reflected the colour of your eyes.

The sky moved across the broken glass, the rain misted and gathered grey fractals together. Spider web anthems span a silent music; I am at a low ebb. The children chose to have icecreams despite the sub-zero weather. The surf is flat, all the answers have gone, there is a ghost at the crossroads, and the cliffs have grown. I am trapped in three dimensions.

She carried the small lacquered box across half the world and for fifty years no-one saw her open it. The sturdy lock survived the interrogations of children, embedded in a picture of birds and a red sky. Occasionally her daughter saw the box next to her bed. When asked, her mother shrugged: 'A keepsake from before the Cultural Revolution.' After her funeral her daughter found a key inside a locket made like a pearl on her mother's necklace, hanging against her breasts. Opening the box caused a momentary hallucination of monkeys screeching in tall trees and a long path wending through bamboo. There was a photograph of a girl with a ponytail, and three letters in an adolescent scrawl—about meeting 'when time is not a dog at a bone.'

though she is a woman now she still needs to be pleasing, pleading, policing because if she skulked around without permission like the vacuous half-baked, half-bearded cunt that followed her, things might be said, set, reset and letters would be sent to editors and complaints made to the management that she'd have to explain away, away, away like a piggy on the run up an arm or over a hill, or coming round the mountain, huff and puff, wee wee wee. oh fly away, you dopey fucker.

He moves at the pace of history; always putting off today what he could do tomorrow: why walk when you can ride? This is the time scale owned by mountains, time as it's played by all who live beyond the reach of needs. Me, I have dishes to wash, dust to sweep up; and when I open the door, slivers of time force themselves inside. No one wants to be outside on a day like this. I wedge the door shut and watch him through a crack in the curtains. Little by little, each vertebra shifts and finds its perfect place. He is fully aware. He is not here. By the time he has reached his full height the storm is here, and the trees are conferring with the wind, arms raised. He raises his arms too, and stands planted on the lawn. His chair matchsticks against the wall, and the branches fall about him with small cries. In the mad flurry he moves, at the pace of history. By the time he has blinked and stretched and taken his first step the storm will be done, and it will be tomorrow, it will be next year.

Night is a dark fabric, torn and patched, that she wears like wings. Star or streetlight, she knows no distinction, each glow bulbing like spittle on lips. Where drops dip and drop, seduced by gravity, they disappear, absorbed in the feathers and fibres. Scab-heeled, she runs down mantled streets, trailing blueblack billows and something like language.

Time doesn't move faster, it just becomes less linear. My grandfather joins me on my walk to the station, carrying a sack of leaf mould and whistling to a dog that died before my father was born. He tells me about a rabbit, hypnotised by a weasel, frozen in sunlight; about his uncle wrestling, winning a watch that isn't even right twice a day. Across the waste ground there are stray cats dancing to the music of steam trains, and there's a gasp as flame pumps a low balloon, voices from the basket clear as metal falling from a wartime sky. When I am young again, I'll climb the fence and run to the tracks, wave at strangers flashing past through smoke-smutted windows, collect names of places I'll one day visit, pick blackberries and catch grasshoppers, maybe fall in love, throw a pebble so high that it'll never come down.

Bitter water, strange bread. He tastes both, thoughtfully, taking his time. What he wants to do is spit them out on the floor but how would that look? Reason stutters out. The water thickens in his mouth. He heard just minutes ago that the king had died and a new world was about to begin. He crumbles bread between his fingers, licks up the crumbs. It tastes like old chalk.

A seagull floats in a spasm of space. I have pieces of wood in sight, holding them at right angles, fitting them together, body and limb. The gull screams and time falls away. I'm holding my father's escaping weight in a hospital bed; I'm caressing the arm of a young woman as my father drinks wine in the next room; I'm being held in my father's arms, sucking my thumb. There are birds above the picnic ground; light makes the sky into a guessing absence. Words between us lift like balloons. I watch them bob and hurry.

They are all reflecting—a circle of mirrors breathing, fingers resting, frames of golden filigree—they take turns keeping the light, the smoke weaves around and between, tinged with cardamom from the morning's coffee—the frames dance to the bells and drums and chaos of traffic below—watch the waves rise and approach, watch an arrow of birds pierce the wind, watch the light blaze and blaze again, watch the reflectors watch the world watching.

Three times a day the train utters its mournful call. Across the river, iron tracks laid a century ago. Don't let's think about who worked those tracks, the picks being swung, the spikes driven in blow by blow, the slip of the hand that left one man shrieking, another lying crushed, red lood on the soil, and the work goes on, and the quake shudders through the spine, the man swinging the hammer under the sun, under the watchman's gaze, the train keeps passing and by 56 cars the children have lost count but still they bounce on their heels, and finally stand quietly as the engine fades into silence, as the train fades into distance, still waving small hands for luck, still watching, as though something significant has passed and, passing, has touched them, has taken some small treasure into the next day.

ACKNOWLEDGMENTS

CASSANDRA ATHERTON:
'It takes a year for the four white stripes on my nails to grow out' was published as 'White Stripes' in *Blackbird Review*, forthcoming 2017.

OWEN BULLOCK:
'Installing' was published in *Uneven Floor* (April 2017).

NILOOFAR FANAIYAN
'Mounds of soil tremble' was published in *Poetry at Sangam* (May 2017).

OZ HARDWICK:
'Time was, you'd fall asleep on trains' was published as part of 'Learning to Have Lost' in *Grief: A Life in 5 Stages 3* (2017).

PAUL MUNDEN:
'Every week' was published in *Stride* and in *The Bulmer Murder* (RWP, 2017).
'You wake' was published in *Cities: Ten Poets, Ten Cities*, ed. S. Strange and P. Hetherington (RWP, 2017).
'Putting it to wash' was published in *Westerly* 61.2 (as 'Kick/Recall') and in *The Bulmer Murder* (RWP, 2017).

ALVIN PANG:
'A British soldier walks out of Grandma's closet' was published in *Cities: Ten Poets, Ten Cities*, ed. S. Strange and P. Hetherington (RWP, 2017).

POEMS/AUTHORS

1	Jen Webb	2	Paul Hetherington
3	Paul Hetherington	4	Shane Strange
5	Paul Hetherington	6	Oz Hardwick
7	Paul Munden	8	Cassandra Atherton
9	Anne Caldwell	10	Rupert Loydell
11	Ross Gibson	12	Jen Webb
13	Alvin Pang	14	Paul Hetherington
15	Jen Webb	16	Penelope Layland
17	Cassandra Atherton	18	Paul Hetherington
19	Paul Munden	20	Andrew Melrose
21	Stephanie Green	22	Oz Hardwick
23	Paul Hetherington	24	Ross Gibson
25	Rupert Loydell	26	Paul Hetherington
27	Cassandra Atherton	28	Rupert Loydell
29	Paul Hetherington	30	Anne Caldwell
31	Jen Webb	32	Oz Hardwick
33	Jordan Williams	34	Jen Webb
35	Cassandra Atherton	36	Monica Carroll
37	Rupert Loydell	38	Penelope Layland
39	Owen Bullock	40	Jen Webb
41	Paul Hetherington	42	Oliver Comins
43	Jen Webb	44	Niloofar Fanaiyan
45	Paul Hetherington	46	Penelope Layland
47	Paul Munden	48	Anne Caldwell
49	Andrew Melrose	50	Jen Webb

51	Paul Hetherington	52	Carrie Etter
53	Stephanie Green	54	Jen Webb
55	Paul Hetherington	56	Oz Hardwick
57	Jen Webb	58	Anne Caldwell
59	Maggie Shapley	60	Jen Crawford
61	Paul Munden	62	Paul Hetherington
63	Jordan Williams	64	Penelope Layland
65	Jen Crawford	66	Rupert Loydell
67	Stephanie Green	68	Anne Caldwell
69	Monica Carroll	70	Alvin Pang
71	Niloofar Fanaiyan	72	Shane Strange
73	Jen Webb	74	Owen Bullock
75	Oz Hardwick	76	Alvin Pang
77	Andrew Melrose	78	Charlotte Guest
79	Niloofar Fanaiyan	80	Oz Hardwick
81	Jen Webb	82	Paul Hetherington
83	Shane Strange	84	Paul Munden
85	Jen Webb	86	Paul Hetherington
87	Jen Webb	88	Oz Hardwick
89	Rupert Loydell	90	Paul Hetherington
91	Shane Strange	92	Jen Webb
93	Oz Hardwick	94	Oz Hardwick
95	Jen Webb	96	Paul Hetherington
97	Niloofar Fanaiyan	98	Jen Webb

BIOGRAPHIES

The PROSE POETRY PROJECT (PPP) was created by the International Poetry Studies Institute (IPSI) in November 2014 with the aim of enabling participants to engage in practice-led research into prose poetry and to write prose poems collegially and collaboratively. The project investigates the form and composition of prose poetry and has yielded both creative and research outcomes. It also explores reasons for the resurgence of interest in the prose poem over recent decades. The Project group has members from Australia, Singapore and the UK, a selection of whom are represented in this anthology.

CASSANDRA ATHERTON is an award-winning writer, academic and critic. She has written thirteen critical and creative books (with two more in progress) and was a Harvard Visiting Scholar in English in 2015/2016. http://cassandra-atherton.com

OWEN BULLOCK'S publications include *River's Edge* (Recent Work Press, 2016), *A Cornish Story* (Palores, 2010) and *sometimes the sky isn't big enough* (Steele Roberts, 2010). He has two new collections forthcoming in 2017: *semi* (Puncher & Wattmann) and *Work & Play* (Recent Work Press). He has edited a number of journals and anthologies, including *Poetry New Zealand*. He recently completed a PhD in Creative Writing at the University of Canberra.

ANNE CALDWELL is a poet, lecturer in Creative Writing at the Open University in the UK and a PhD student at the University of Bolton. Her latest poetry collection is *Painting the Spiral Staircase* (Cinnamon, 2016). blog: http://annecaldwell.net

MONICA CARROLL holds a PhD in philosophy and poetry from the University of Canberra. She is a Creative and Cultural Fellow for the Centre for Creative and Cultural Research. Her creative work has been celebrated with many international and national awards. She recently co-edited *Tremble* (2016) through the International Poetry Studies Institute, *Pulse* (2016) with Recent Works Press and a special issue of *TEXT* 'Making it New: Finding contemporary meanings for creativity'.

JEN CRAWFORD'S poetry publications include *Admissions* (Five Islands Press, 2000), *Bad Appendix* (Titus Books, 2008), *Pop Riveter* (Pania Press, 2011) and *Koel* (Cordite Books, 2016). She is an Assistant Professor of Creative Writing at the University of Canberra.

OLIVER COMINS lives and works in West London. Two short collections (*Yes to Everything* and *Staying in Touch*) won Templar Poetry Pamphlet Awards. A third (*Battling Against the Odds*) is about the game of golf and the sport of life and has led to the author's appointment as UK National Golf Month Poet.

CARRIE ETTER is a Reader in Creative Writing at Bath Spa University. She has published three collections: *The Tethers* (Seren, 2009), *Divining for Starters* (Shearsman, 2011), and *Imagined Sons* (Seren, 2014). She edited

Infinite Difference: Other Poetries by UK Women Poets (Shearsman, 2010) and Linda Lamus's posthumous collection, *A Crater the Size of Calcutta* (Mulfran, 2015). Her fourth collection, *The Weather in Normal*, will be published by Seren in 2018.

NILOOFAR FANAIYAN is a poet, writer, and researcher. She has a PhD in creative writing from the University of Canberra and was the 2016 Donald Horne Fellow at the Centre for Creative and Cultural Research. She received the 2016 Canberra Critics Circle Literary Award for Poetry for her book of poems titled *Transit*.

ROSS GIBSON is Centenary Professor in the Faculty of Arts & Design at the University of Canberra. His books include *Changescapes* (2015) and *Memoryscopes* (2015) published by UWAP. His most recent collection of poetry is *Stone Grown Cold* (2015) published by Cordite Books.

STEPHANIE GREEN is a cultural historian, a widely published essayist and fiction writer. She is Deputy Head of School at Griffith University's School of Humanities, Languages and Social Science and her most recently published research is on women in transmedia narrative.

CHARLOTTE GUEST is a Western Australian writer and Publishing Officer at UWA Publishing. Her work has appeared in *Griffith Review*, *Overland*, *Australian Book Review*, *Westerly Magazine*, *Cordite*, *Voiceworks*, *Writ Poetry Review* and elsewhere.

OZ HARDWICK is a writer, photographer, music journalist, and occasional musician, based in York (UK). His sixth poetry collection, *The House of Ghosts and Mirrors*, will be published by Valley Press in September 2017. In a parallel existence, Oz is also Professor of English at Leeds Trinity University, and has written extensively on misericords and animal iconography in the Middle Ages under the pseudonym of Paul Hardwick. www.ozhardwick.co.uk

PAUL HETHERINGTON has published eleven full-length collections of poetry, most recently *Burnt Umber* (UWAP, 2016) and *Gallery of Antique Art* (RWP, 2016). He won the 2014 Western Australian Premier's Book Awards (poetry) and undertook an Australia Council for the Arts Literature Board Residency at the BR Whiting Studio in Rome in 2015-16. He is Professor of Writing and head of the International Poetry Studies Institute at the University of Canberra.

PENELOPE LAYLAND has published two books of poetry: *The Unlikely Orchard* (Molonglo Books) and *Suburban Anatomy* (Pandanus Books). She has worked as a journalist, speechwriter and as a communications professional.

RUPERT LOYDELL is Senior Lecturer in the School of Writing and Journalism at Falmouth University, a writer, editor and abstract artist. He has many books of poetry in print, including the recently published *Dear Mary* (Shearsman, 2017).

ANDREW MELROSE is Professor of Children's Writing at the University of Winchester, UK. He has over 150 film, fiction, non-fiction, research, songs, poems and other writing credits, including 33 scholarly or creative books. He is currently working on *The Boat* an extended poem, book and exhibition about people migrating to safer countries on boats http://theimmigration-boat-story.com

PAUL MUNDEN is Postdoctoral Research Fellow (Poetry & Creative Practice) at the University of Canberra. He is General Editor of *Writing in Education* and *Writing in Practice*, both published by the National Association of Writers in Education (NAWE), of which he is Director. His latest collection of poetry is *Chromatic*, to be published by UWAP in October 2017.

ALVIN PANG is a poet, writer and editor based in Singapore, but active in literary practice worldwide. Among his many engagements, he is a member of the IPSI Advisory Board. Author of over a dozen books, his poetry has been translated into more than twenty languages.

MAGGIE SHAPLEY is a Canberra poet and University Archivist at the Australian National University. She won the 2003 ACT Writers Centre Poetry Award and her poems have been published in literary journals, anthologies and on Canberra buses as co-winners of the Poetry in Action Prize 2007 to 2009.

SHANE STRANGE is a doctoral candidate and Teaching Fellow in the Faculty of Arts and Design at the University of Canberra and an HDR member of the Faculty's Centre for Creative and Cultural Research (CCCR). He tutors and lectures in Writing and Literary Studies. His writing has been published widely in Australia.

JEN WEBB is a writer and cultural theorist, and Director of the Centre for Creative and Cultural Research at the University of Canberra. She writes poetry, researches creative practice, and makes and exhibits artist books. Her most recent books are *Watching the World* (with Paul Hetherington) and *Researching Creative Writing*.

JORDAN WILLIAMS is Associate Professor of Writing at the University of Canberra. She pursues an ongoing interest in the future directions of reading and writing including new forms such as new-media writing as well as the growing popularity of older forms such as the graphic novel, and the nexus between fiction and non-fiction.

2016 Editions

Pulse Prose Poetry Project
Incantations Subhash Jaireth
Transit Niloofar Fanaiyan
Gallery of Antique Art Paul Hetherington
Sentences from the Archive Jen Webb
River's Edge Owen Bullock

2017 Editions

A Song, the World to Come Miranda Lello
Members Only Melinda Smith & Caren Florance
the future: un-imagine Angela Gardner & Caren Florance
Cities: Ten Poets, Ten Cities Various
The Bulmer Murder Paul Munden
Dew and Broken Glass Penny Drysdale
Proof Maggie Shapley
Black Tulips Moya Pacey
Soap Charlotte Guest
Isolator Monica Carroll
Ikaros Paul Hetherington
Work & Play Owen Bullock

all titles available from
recentworkpress.com

www.ingramcontent.com/pod-product-compliance
Lightning Source LLC
Chambersburg PA
CBHW020619300426
44113CB00007B/710